Preparing For Divorce: Financial Health Assessment
Do-it-Yourself Workbook

This book can be purchased in bulk at a wholesale discount via IngramSpark. It is also available internationally via Amazon.com.

Publisher: Unfold Your Success, LLC
Paperback ISBN: 978-0-578-51765-0

Contact Audra McMahon at:
Email: Audra@AudraMcMahon.com | Audra@Option29.org
Web: AudraMcMahon.com | Option29.org

Credits:
Cover Design, Interior Layout & Design: Gagan Sarkaria, M.F.A., M.B.A.
https://GaganSarkaria.com | https://UnfoldYourSuccess.com
Branding, Marketing Copy & Content Writing: Gagan Sarkaria

Preparing for Divorce

FINANCIAL HEALTH

Assessment

Audra McMahon, CMPS, CDLP

Separating Emotion From Logic

Preparing for Divorce
FINANCIAL HEALTH
Assessment

TABLE OF CONTENTS

Do-it-Yourself Workbook

This Workbook Belongs to:

Name:	

PRAISE FOR *Preparing for Divorce* FINANCIAL HEALTH Assessment

Audra truly cares about your well-being and has the best contacts and resources available for anyone going through a divorce. She helped me find and buy a home after my divorce, and personalized all of her messages to me, making me feel like one of a kind. Can't wait to work with her again in the future!
— Billy Kittle

For those who are divorcing, Audra's Option29.org is essential for a good, healthy outcome. I highly recommend her services.
— Martha Patton Childers

I have worked with Audra McMahon for close to 10 years. She earned my business by being impeccable with her word. She has a solid understanding of finance and the ability to quickly determine what programs our clients can work with. Audra's word is like gold. I can count on it. That's not the standard in business, so she is a shining light! On top of her stellar performance professionally, she has the biggest heart in the world. She is right in the trenches with our clients and guiding them mentally, emotionally, and spiritually. Her high energy, bubbly person-

ality, combined with the love of geeking out the number crunching and embracing the human experience through the emotional roller coaster ride of life, causes Audra to be unparalleled in her industry. I consider myself fortunate to have her as my friend and business partner.
— Paul A. Skehen

The workbook provided me peace of mind in a time where I needed clarity. I had logical steps to follow to prepare myself for whatever meetings I would have. It was a great tool to feel productive while feeling powerless. It boiled an overwhelming process into manageable steps. Highly recommend investing in yourself by purchasing this book!
— Marie N.

It has been a labor of pain and pure joy, seeing this workbook come to life. I have known Audra for almost 5 years now. She is a thorough professional, super smart with money, mortgage, and guiding and teaching you how to successfully manage Divorce's minutia. Audra understands the pain of going through a Divorce. She excels in separating emotion from logic, giving you a unique perspective through her coaching, consulting, and through this workbook. I genuinely believe this workbook is an enlightening tool for clarity and preparedness. This workbook offers a clear, in-depth, and a holistic approach to assessing your financial health, during significant transitions in your relationship.
— Gagan Sarkaria, High Achievement Book, Branding & Business Coach

"Quality means doing it right when no one is looking.

—Henry Ford, Amercian Businessman

“Determination gives you the resolve to keep going in spite of the roadblocks that lay before you.

—Denis Waitley, American Writer

DEDICATION

This book is dedicated to all the people I have known who have struggled to break free from painful and often abusive marriages. Your courage and determination have inspired me not only to complete this endeavor but also to support various families to transition — from having two parents to one parent — successfully, boldly, and lovingly.

If you are struggling to navigate your transition during divorce, you are not alone. **This book is dedicated to you.**

I never want anyone to feel the same horror, confusion, insecurity, I felt when I went through a divorce. I genuinely want to protect you. Knowledge is power, and this workbook is just the next step in the right direction.

“Nothing in life is to be feared, it is only to be understood. Now is the time to understand more, so that we may fear less.

—Marie Curie, Polish Scientist

ACKNOWLEDGEMENTS

This workbook, **Preparing For Divorce: Financial Health Assessment Do-it-yourself Workbook,** and Option29.org programs and services are a result of years of helping many. I am fortunate to serve, guide, and ease my clients' pain of separation, agony, fear, and lack of security. In some cases, **have a wake-up call** to rebuild relationships and recommit to redesign their marriage.

For this workbook, I acknowledge my ex-husband, Aaron. If we had not divorced, I would not have gone down this path of continuous search to stop the pain, anxiety, and fear. I thank him for being the catalyst that pushed me to embark on my personal journey to find the hidden gems along the way!

My biggest treasure is my daughter, Mary Grace. Another one is Option29.org, through which my team and I continue to serve many families and individuals going through the similar pain I went through. I know there is a solution to the hardships, struggles, fears, and pain. We have to be courageous enough to **separate the emotion from the logic.** This is where this do-it-yourself workbook guides you, step-by-step, how to do the same.

CHAPTER 1

FINANCIAL OVERVIEW

CHAPTER ONE

Document All The Money Coming In

Before we look at the earnings, please answer the following questions:

- Is there an existing prenuptial agreement?
- Have you been served divorce papers?
- Have you filed for divorce?

As you begin, the only way you will get through this assessment is, to be honest, open, and willing. You can do it. Here's to clarifying your current life position, so you can see the next best step for you and your life! Let's begin.

In this chapter, you'll need to search every penny that comes to you annually, and each penny you have spent in the last 3 months.

MONEY COMING IN:

Your job, your passive income, tax returns, gifts, inheritance, and interest income. The easiest and the best way to do this is to first look at your tax returns and discern where the money has come from. Then do a quick glance at your bank account for all deposits. Scan them over, and there you have an accounting of all pennies coming into your life.

Now, remember, if you're like me and share my personal mantra, "money flows to me like water flows to the ocean," you'll want to make space for FOUND money. My daughter and I pick up change, and find about $300 per year in cash that was not expected because we expect the unexpected!

For this chapter, you'll need your tax returns and online access to your bank account to log in and quickly search your statements for deposits. You've got this! It's fun to see where your money comes from!

Remember to complete your gratitude journaling pages at the end of this chapter and really give thanks for each stream of income coming to your life. In looking at this money, you may begin to notice a lack of funds. That's okay. Take this moment to really think about what you want in your life. In your journaling, get specific about what you'd like to attract and create income-wise. Perhaps it's time to find a new job, ask for that raise, create a side hustle with a passive stream of income that you never thought of before. Listen to your gut. That's your connection to the world talking to you, through you. Believe it or not, you already know precisely what you need. You just have to create a space to access it!

LIST ITEMS	PARTNER 1	PARTNER 2	JOINT
Base Salary	$	$	$
Commissions (2-yr Average)	$	$	$
Overtime (2-yr Average)	$	$	$
Bonus (Work-related; 2-yr Average)	$		$
Gambling	$	$	$
Gifts From Others (IRS Compliant)	$	$	$
Settlements	$	$	$
Alimony (Pre-vious Relation-ships)	$	$	$
Child Support	$	$	$
Retirement	$	$	$
State Issued Income or Support (SS, Disability, Food Stamps)	$	$	$
Any Income Reported on Taxes (Rental Property, Farm, etc.)	$	$	$

LIST ITEMS	PARTNER 1	PARTNER 2	JOINT
Cash From Unknown, Undocumented Sources	$	$	$
Tax Refund	$	$	$
	$	$	$
	$	$	$
	$	$	$
	$	$	$
	$	$	$
	$	$	$
	$	$	$
Total Income Received	$	$	$

COUNTING MY BLESSINGS

My Personal Gratitude Journal

I AM GRATEFUL FOR	I WANT TO ATTRACT

WHAT I LIKE ABOUT MYSELF TODAY

SURRENDER – WHAT DO I NEED TO RELEASE TODAY?

ACTION STEPS TO TAKE

"Education is the key to unlocking the world, a passport to freedom.

– Oprah Winfrey

CHAPTER 2

DEBITS

CHAPTER TWO

Document All The Money Going Out

Alright, this section of the workbook may be the most confronting if you're not actively keeping a budget, and balancing your checkbook daily. Take a breath. Expect some human resistance to even getting this done. As you begin this section, you'll need to set aside a couple hours to get this done effectively. Remember, what you give is what you get here. The data will only be as accurate as you detail it. Choosing to skip steps will leave you with an inaccurate picture of your actual spending.

Gather your most recent 3 months of bank statements and credit card statements. Categorize each penny, TO THE PENNY. Do not round up what you have spent. If you have a coffee habit that costs you $3500 a month, write it down, and be honest about it. There is nothing wrong with spending your money how you want to spend your money. Now, if it doesn't work for you, meaning, you're spending more than you save, and going into debt each month, then a change needs to come. Taking note of it now is the first step. If you don't know, you can't create what you want. You can't manage what you don't monitor.

Once you define your spending, you'll be fully aware of where you are, and you will have a visceral or physical reaction to this meeting the expectations of your life or not. Keep going. You're not bad or wrong. These are only numbers of past activities. Gather the data.

Itemize, and average your last 3 months of spending. Write the totals of those averages here. Add any category you need that has not been suggested that you find from reviewing your bank and credit card statements (again, coffee, booze, technology, shopping, games, gambling, clubs, Amazon, Target/Walmart/Costco/Sams). It's crucial to discern eating in vs. eating out, so you can get present to your eating behaviors. For those stores where you can buy all things, and cannot separate if you purchased food, clothing, household swag, etc., make a new category for that store itself. If your expense cannot be broken down into food, home repair, gardening, clothes, etc., you categorize it within itself. If the average spending does not work for your financial life — you make a change.

If you find yourself stuck here, you may need a coach to walk you through it. You're not alone. People hire us exclusively to just examine this portion of their life because the task is overwhelming. That's okay. If you find yourself getting stuck, just call, and we'll do it together. Check out our additional services referenced later in this book for ways Option29.org can help you on this journey.

No one will see the details of this process, but you (unless you share it), so be honest and accurate. Avoiding the legitimate facts about where you have already spent your money is only going to hurt your future financial freedom. If your debts are higher than your income, and you don't know what to do about it, call us to get some tips, or contact your trusted financial advisor.

LIST ITEMS	PARTNER 1	PARTNER 2	FAMILY
House mortgage (includes Escrow: yes/no)	$	$	$
Home equity	$	$	$
Car 1	$	$	$
Car 2	$	$	$
Personal Loans	$	$	$
Student Loans	$	$	$
Credit Card Payments	$	$	$
Store Credit Card Payments	$	$	$
Other debt	$	$	$
Taxes (personal property tax (home/vehicle) annual divided into monthly)	$	$	$
Electric (equal-pay or budget billing: yes/no)	$	$	$
Natural Gas	$	$	$
Water/Sewer/Trash/Refuse/Recycling	$	$	$
SUBTOTAL 1			

LIST ITEMS	PARTNER 1	PARTNER 2	FAMILY
Phone & Cellular	$	$	$
Groceries	$	$	$
Gasoline/Cars	$	$	$
Netflix	$	$	$
Cable/Internet	$	$	$
Entertainment (Eating out/Movies, Social events, etc.)	$	$	$
Habits (Alcohol, Wine, Smoking, etc.)	$	$	$
Secrets (Other Substance, gambling, other activities)	$	$	$
Unknown Cash Withdrawals	$	$	$
Clothing	$	$	$
Shoes	$	$	$
Hair	$	$	$
Nails	$	$	$
Vanity (Other)	$	$	$
Charities	$	$	$
SUBTOTAL 2			

LIST ITEMS	PARTNER 1	PARTNER 2	FAMILY
Health & Fitness	$	$	$
Childcare	$	$	$
Child(ren) Activities	$	$	$
Child(ren) Allowance	$	$	$
Education	$	$	$
Personal Development	$	$	$
Books	$	$	$
Social Networking	$	$	$
Medical	$	$	$
Nutritional	$	$	$
Pet Needs (Medical, Grooming, Daycare)	$	$	$
Memberships/ Subscriptions	$	$	$
Sports	$	$	$
Magazines	$	$	$
Donations	$	$	$
Clubs	$	$	$
SUBTOTAL 3			
Add all 3 subtotals for Total Monthly Expenses	$	$	$

LIST ITEMS	PARTNER 1	PARTNER 2	FAMILY
	$	$	$
	$	$	$
	$	$	$
	$	$	$
	$	$	$
	$	$	$
	$	$	$
	$	$	$
	$	$	$
	$	$	$
	$	$	$
	$	$	$
	$	$	$
	$	$	$
	$	$	$
	$	$	$
	$	$	$
	$	$	$
	$	$	$
Total Monthly Expenses	$	$	$

INSURANCE/SAVINGS

List Monthly Contributions

LIST ITEMS	PARTNER 1	PARTNER 2	FAMILY
Home Owner's Insurance (If not included in mortgage escrow)	$	$	$
Car Insurance (Number of Cars ____)	$	$	$
Life Insurance (Individuals Covered ____)	$	$	$
Health Insurance (Individuals Covered ____)	$	$	$
Dental Insurance (Individuals Covered ____)	$	$	$
Vision Insurance (Individuals Covered ____)	$	$	$
Short-term Savings (Emergency Fund)	$	$	$
Long-term Savings (Goals)	$	$	$
Other Savings (Retirement not taken from pay)	$	$	$
Total Monthly Contributions	$	$	$

Let's Add it All:

TOTAL INCOME (FROM PAGE 20, END OF CH 1):

TOTAL EXPENSES (FROM PAGES 27 TO 31, CH 2):

DISPOSABLE INCOME (TOTAL INCOME MINUS DEBTS = MONEY REMAINING AT THE END OF THE MONTH)

Considering that you have accurately accounted for each penny, if this disposable income does not match your savings contribution or isn't $0, you have room for improvement. Learning to better manage your daily spending will serve you more. You may consider seeking help through our additional services with your Money Mindset.

CRUCIAL QUESTIONS:

Answer the following:

What surfaced when you sat back and looked at your life?

During your review, what things on a daily, weekly, monthly, and annual basis became clear that cost you money?

Take notes of the legal description of your debts (vehicles and homes). Your attorney will need those. There is space in this workbook for that data in the following chapters.

Now, take a break. Remember to breathe. Come back and look at this again. If you're not sure about something, make a note to discern the facts about what already is. This section is to look at what is typical in your financial life. You're not splitting things up yet. Just gathering facts. Pretend like you're looking at something that is not yours, and just get to it! You CAN do it. Be like Nike®, and just do it!

COUNTING MY BLESSINGS

My Personal Gratitude Journal

I AM GRATEFUL FOR	I WANT TO ATTRACT

WHAT I LIKE ABOUT MYSELF TODAY

SURRENDER – WHAT DO I NEED TO RELEASE TODAY?

ACTION STEPS TO TAKE

"You cannot always control what goes on outside. But you can control what goes on the inside.

– Yogic principle

CHAPTER 3

MONEY ACCOUNTS

CHAPTER THREE

In this chapter, we are going to focus on listing all the accounts, and items that have money with your name on them. These could be individual, personal accounts, joint accounts, tangible items, and accounts where your partner is the primary account holder.

You should know what accounts you have, but you may not know precisely what your partner has in the personal or business bank accounts. If you have asked direct questions and been met with resistance, or received an ambiguous response, and **your instinct** is telling you something is off, it likely is. **Can you answer these questions:**

- Do you see cash withdrawals from your bank statements that you didn't know about or discuss, yet your partner doesn't seem to have cash?
- Are you sharing a joint checking/savings, but the money being deposited into that account doesn't match the salary your partner is being paid?
- Do you have an instinctive message coming that something's not right? Always wondering where our money is? Your partner may have an addictive problem or be funneling money somewhere else, without your knowledge.

If you're worried about your partner having abusive behaviors, you may need to reach out for help. If you're noticing less money showing up in your accounts, and your partner denies any such activity, you may need to express this to an attorney. Engaging a forensic accountant in your legal proceedings may serve you better. Your attorney will be able to guide you here.

Note: If you are to the point where you have already filed divorce, and are using this workbook for personal clarity, you have forfeited the right to openly discuss your partner's money from the date they left your relationship. It might be prudent to let the attorneys handle your questions of perceived missing funds. Don't ignore your instincts.

Additional Note: On tangible items that are of emotional value to you, please understand that any commodity is only worth what a potential buyer is willing to pay in the market today. For example, your home may have been worth $500K when you purchased it. Still, during an economic recession, the house may decrease in value. You may take a loss from that initial purchase price when selling. Also, take into consideration that there will be fees for determining the value of any commodity you wish to sell and unforeseen costs. Therefore, have an **appropriate third-party representation** to sell that commodity.

LIST ITEMS	PARTNER 1	PARTNER 2	JOINT
Checking	$	$	$
Savings	$	$	$
Money Market	$	$	$
CD(s)	$	$	$
Stocks	$	$	$
Bonds	$	$	$
Annuities	$	$	$
Retirement	$	$	$
Vehicles	$	$	$
Homes	$	$	$
Antiques	$	$	$
Jewelry	$	$	$
Home Values	$	$	$
Allowance	$	$	$
Total Amount			

DETAILS OF TANGIBLE ITEMS

List items paid-in-full over $100

LIST ITEMS	VALUE
	$
	$
	$
	$
	$
	$
	$
	$
	$
	$
	$
	$
	$
	$
	$
	$
	$
	$
SUBTOTAL 1	$

LIST ITEMS	VALUE
	$
	$
	$
	$
	$
	$
	$
	$
	$
	$
	$
	$
	$
	$
	$
	$
	$
	$
	$
	$
	$
SUBTOTAL 2	$
TOTAL (SUBTOTALS 1+2)	$

"Don't stop when you're tired.
Stop when you're done.

—Marilyn Monroe, American Actress

COUNTING MY BLESSINGS

My Personal Gratitude Journal

I AM GRATEFUL FOR	I WANT TO ATTRACT

WHAT I LIKE ABOUT MYSELF TODAY

SURRENDER – WHAT DO I NEED TO RELEASE TODAY?

ACTION STEPS TO TAKE

“When written in Chinese, the word ‘crisis’ is composed of two characters. One represents danger and the other represents opportunity.

–John F. Kennedy, 35th President of the United States of America

CHAPTER 4

TO-DO LISTS

CHAPTER FOUR

Now, we are going to get geared up to take some action-steps. We will start with some crucial to-do lists below. These are suggestions that have been very beneficial to our clients in setting new boundaries that work. If taking action in the following tips does not feel appropriate, listen to your inner guidance.

IDENTITY

Protecting Your Most Valuable Asset

IDENTITY ITEMS	ADVICE	√
2-Factor Authentication	Set it up for all Online accounts	
Modes of Communication	Make a list of all places where password is needed	
Phone	Who controls the children's phone?	

IDENTITY ITEMS	ADVICE	√
Burner app	Look into for privacy if safety is a concern https://www.burnerapp.com/	
Emails:	Change password • Work: Ensure no access on joint computer • Personal: create a new account and only share with your attorney	
All Social Media Accounts	HIBERNATE. Limit your presence on social media, and make all your accounts PRIVATE. You having fun, even with your children, can cause your partner emotional aggravation during a divorce. Our experience shows it causes difficulty in creating win-win environments at all stages of an unsettled relationship.	
Name Change	Do you want to change your name? Is this important to how you identify with yourself, your family, your community?	

IDENTITY ITEMS	ADVICE	√
Driver's License	Note expiration and name. Locate your original.	
Passport	Note expiration and name. Locate your original. Same for minor dependents.	
Social Security Card	This is the first change before your other forms of identification can be altered. Locate your original.	
Birth Certificates	Locate your original.	
Marriage Certificte	Locate your original.	
Educational Certificates & Degrees	Locate your original.	
Memorabilia	Share and/or copy it to a drive for your new private email.	
Photo Albums	Contact a local company that can digitize your hard copy original memories.	
Discs	Identify all discs, and make copies as needed.	

TIP: We suggest getting an external hard drive for all tangible memories.

YOUR NETWORK

Write Name, Phone & Email Addresses

NETWORK	NAME & PHONE	EMAIL
CPA		
CMPS		
CDFA		
Attorney • Family • Business • Other known attorneys		
Business Coach		
Life Coach		

NETWORK	NAME & PHONE	EMAIL
Mentor		
Pastor		
Insurance Agent		
Realtor		
Counselor/ Therapist		
Job Placement Agency Contact		
Nanny		
Maid Service		

NETWORK	NAME & PHONE	EMAIL
Handy Man		
Assistant (Virtual)		
Small Groups		
House Helpers • Lawn • Pool • Gardner • Pest Control • Gutter Cleaner • Window Cleaner		

"Time takes time.

—Anonymous

PERSONAL SUPPORT SYSTEM

Family, Friends, Neighbors, Emergency Contacts

NETWORK	NAME & PHONE	EMAIL

ACTION ITEMS

Document Details of Action Steps to Take

Reflect on your life right now. What do you need? What are you currently experiencing? What tendencies, urges, and cravings are you aware of? Jot that down in each section under the details of these critical tasks.

IMPORTANT TASKS	DETAILS
Divorce decree requirements, if already served	
Emotional Needs	

IMPORTANT TASKS	DETAILS
Prescription Medications	
Natural Supplements	
Genetic Tendencies	
Mental Health (Depression, Anxiety, Insomnia, etc.)	

IMPORTANT TASKS	DETAILS
Energy Healing (Reiki, Shamanic work, Age-regression, Hypnotherapy, Inner-child work, etc.)	
Therapy • Individual • Child(ren) • Family	
Support Groups	

IMPORTANT TASKS	DETAILS
Alcoholism	
Alcoholics Anonymous (AA)	
Al-Anon & Alateen	
Narcotics Anonymous (NA)	
National Suicide Prevention Hotline	

PHYSICAL NEEDS

Document Details of Your Physical Needs

PHYSICAL NEEDS	DETAILS
Diet & Nutrition	
Massage	
Hormones Testing & Therapy	
DNA Testing (Check out variety of self-initiated DNA tests with home kits for health & wellness*)	

PHYSICAL NEEDS	DETAILS
Dental Needs	
Pre-existing Medical Needs	
Sleep	
Exercise	
Annual physical check ups	

CRITICAL INFO SHEET CHECKLIST

Document Details of Action Steps to Take

CRITICAL CHECKLIST	INFORMATION
• Call 911 if in danger	
• Locate a non-emergency phone number for the nearest police department	
• Pack a safe bag with cash to be away for a weekend. Keep some change of clothes and a toothbrush in the trunk of your car, one for each member of your household, that you believe could potentially be in danger.	
• Make a private escape plan	
• Make 1 person a CONFIDENTIAL safe person	
• Change locks	
• Alarm (get one with video at door)	
• Know when to call the police	
• Bodyguards	
• Create a health care directive	

CRITICAL CHECKLIST	INFORMATION
• Make a list of assets, and a copy of your legal documents	
• Update will	
• Update estate	
• Update trust	
• Provide copy of documents to trustees and beneficiaries	
• Provide title to successors	
• Communication with children's educational facility/ daycare	
• Parenting plan	
• Copy of parenting plan to school/people that help with children	
• Copy of documents uploaded to new email private drive	
• Community resources	
• Spiritual resources	
• Church affiliation	
~ Religious denomination	
~ Annulment	
~ Small groups	

“Happiness is internal, and joy is an external concept. We often seek both in our environment from others. Manage your mind. Take charge of your inner happiness, and let joy flow to you.

–Gagan Sarkaria, High Achievement Life & Business Coach

"The secret of getting ahead is getting started.

—Mark Twain, American Author

COUNTING MY BLESSINGS

My Personal Gratitude Journal

I AM GRATEFUL FOR	I WANT TO ATTRACT

WHAT I LIKE ABOUT MYSELF TODAY

SURRENDER – WHAT DO I NEED TO RELEASE TODAY?

ACTION STEPS TO TAKE

"My mission in life is not merely to survive, but to thrive; and to do so with some passion, some compassion, some humor, and some style.

–Maya Angelou, American Poet

CHAPTER 5

PERSONAL GOALS

CHAPTER FIVE

As you look at your life, it might be hard to imagine a future without your current partner. This chapter will help you realign with your personal values — financially, spiritually, emotionally, and physically. The question to ask yourself is, no matter where I am in my relationship with my partner, what do I want personally for my life as if I am the only one who will always be in it? No other humans, guaranteed. It's a brutal thought.

For example, let's say I am on the fence with getting a divorce or not, and I've purchased this workbook to take a look at my whole life. **In one month, I may want:**

Physically – to start sleeping 8 hours a night again.

Mentally – schedule an appointment with my therapist, or find a new coach/counselor to talk through what's bothering me.

Spiritually – join a group that aligns with my beliefs and supports them.

Financially – ask for that raise that I've wanted to ask about for the past 3 years but haven't, and create a new budget that works for my financial future as it is right now.

In 3 months, those goals are met, and now my new goals are:
Physically – start walking 3 miles a day.
Mentally – begin a meditation and journaling routine to gain clarity.
Spiritually – I am confident to choose to stay in my relationship or leave it in divorce.
Financially – I have saved 3 months of my monthly bills, and keep a regular budget that I monitor weekly.

Keep going from there! Just picture yourself meeting these goals, step back, and create the life you want to design! Now is the time to write down your goals — physical, financial, emotional, spiritual and legal. Let's break them down to short-term and long-term goals. For your goals in 24 and 60 months, DREAM BIG. BE LIMITLESS. Write out something for your life that you think is impossible today, yet you would love to look that way when the time comes.

1-month goals:

PHYSICAL

MENTAL/EMOTIONAL

SPIRITUAL

FINANCIAL

3-month goals:

PHYSICAL

MENTAL/EMOTIONAL

SPIRITUAL

FINANCIAL

6-month goals:

PHYSICAL

MENTAL/EMOTIONAL

SPIRITUAL

FINANCIAL

12-month goals:

PHYSICAL

MENTAL/EMOTIONAL

SPIRITUAL

FINANCIAL

24-month goals:

PHYSICAL

MENTAL/EMOTIONAL

SPIRITUAL

FINANCIAL

36-month goals:

PHYSICAL

MENTAL/EMOTIONAL

SPIRITUAL

FINANCIAL

60-month goals:

PHYSICAL

MENTAL/EMOTIONAL

SPIRITUAL

FINANCIAL

“Whether you think you can or think you can’t, you’re right.

—Henry Ford

COUNTING MY BLESSINGS

My Personal Gratitude Journal

I AM GRATEFUL FOR	I WANT TO ATTRACT

WHAT I LIKE ABOUT MYSELF TODAY

SURRENDER – WHAT DO I NEED TO RELEASE TODAY?

ACTION STEPS TO TAKE

"You must be the change you wish to see in the world.

–Mahatama Gandhi

CHAPTER 6

CRITICAL CHECKLIST

CHAPTER SIX

Do you have the following information accessible? If not, make sure you gather these and check them off as you have collect them. These are the **actual documents** that you will want to have prepared for your first **meeting with your attorney.** The longer you take in gathering this data, and the more you hand-holding you need to provide this support, the higher your legal bills will be.

Remember, your attorney bills hourly. **Gain clarity on their costs before you sign a contract.** Gather this data and the questions you have in this workbook, and you'll be a dream client who chances are, they will help first and fast because of your preparation!

CHECKLIST	INFO ACCESSIBLE YES/NO
12 months of Asset Statements **• Checking** **• Savings** **• Retirement** **• Stocks** **• Bonds** **• CD** **• Money Markets**	

CHECKLIST	INFO ACCESSIBLE YES/NO
Checking	
Savings	
Retirement	
Stocks/Bonds?CDs/MMAs	
3 years of Tax Returns	
Personal & Business	
YTD Profit & Loss	
YTD Balance Sheet	
3 years of W2s and K1s	
Year-End Pay Stubs from the previous year	
30 days of pay stubs	
Mortgage statements for all properties owned	
Special Assessments for all properties	
HOA dues for all properties	
Costs to run home (see budget in chapter 2, and itemize for each property)	
Insurance Declaration page for all properties owned	
Copy of ID	
List of vehicles owned with VIN	

CHECKLIST	INFO ACCESSIBLE YES/NO
Vehicle Insurance Policies	
Life Insurance Policies	
Divorce Decree (if applicable)	
Child Support Guideline from your state (if applicable)	
Property Settlement Statement (if applicable)	
List of your concerns	

“Learn from yesterday, live for today, hope for tomorrow. The important thing is not to stop questioning.

—Albert Einstein, German Physicst

COUNTING MY BLESSINGS

My Personal Gratitude Journal

I AM GRATEFUL FOR	I WANT TO ATTRACT

WHAT I LIKE ABOUT MYSELF TODAY

SURRENDER – WHAT DO I NEED TO RELEASE TODAY?

ACTION STEPS TO TAKE

"Let your yes mean yes, and your no mean no.

–Matthew 5:37

CHAPTER 7

HOLISTIC HEALING

RESOURCES: CHAPTER SEVEN

I believe in healing the Mind, Body, and Soul for a better, healthier, royal you. Often, during times of stress, the first thing we ignore is our bodies. Remember, our bodies keep a score of every pain, every trauma, every discomfort, which later can surface as a dis-ease of the body. I highly recommend that you do not ignore these aspects of your holistic, beautiful being.

Below are some of my recommendations as you gather the courage to rediscover, refine, reestablish yourself. Keep these resources and recommendations handy — you will need them. Take any and all activities on at your own discretion and risk. Please consider talking to your health care provider.

HEALING THE BODY

I have divided this section into six subcategories: food, exercise, alternative therapies, relaxation tools and techniques, books, and movies and documentaries.

Food:

Watch what you eat, when you eat, how you eat, and why you eat it. Remember, food is a giver. It gives you nutrition, health, and healing. You've got to treat food with love, kindness, and respect — like you do your elders, doctors, and healthcare providers. Below is some food-for-thought as you begin your healing journey.

- Diet
- Vitamins
- Food combining
- A Macrobiotic diet
- Natural herbs & mineral supplements
- Bach Flower Remedies (BFRs)
- Homeopathy
- Ayurvedic lifestyle
- Natural detoxification processes
- Healing with herbal teas
- Chakra healing foods

Exercise:

Shawn Achor, the bestselling author of the book, The Happiness Advantage, once said, "When people exercise, we talk about endorphins, but endorphins are just short-term. Exercise is valuable because it trains your brain to believe, 'My behavior matters,' which is optimism." So yes, you need the endorphins and the confidence in your body! Below are some of my suggestions:

- Walking
- Dancing
- Bike riding
- Cycling
- Yoga

- Pilates
- Aerobics
- Jazzercise
- Trampoline activities
- Tai Chi
- Martial arts
- Swimming
- Sports
- Hire a personal trainer and develop a routine specifically designed for you!

Integrative Medicine and Alternative Therapies:

Integrative health is a patient-centered approach that includes all medical and healthcare professions — conventional, alternative, Asian, Eastern, natural, and holistic. Below is a list that you may look into as you follow your intuition and research around these concepts.

- Massage and Bodywork
- Reiki Healing
- Qi Gong
- Acupuncture
- Acupressure
- Colon therapy
- Naturopathy
- Functional Medicine
- Chiropractic Medicine
- Ayurvedic Medicine
- Herbal Medicine
- Reflexology
- Chromotherapy
- Aromatherapy
- Bioenergetics

- Heart-centered Hypnotherapy® as offered by wellness-institute.org certified practitioners & graduates
- EMDR therapy
- Deep tissue work

Relaxation Tools & Techniques:

One of my favorite tools for relaxation, stress management, and better sleep is called PSiO. It is a pair of hi-tech light and sound therapy glasses with audible programs that you can customize to your needs. There are mediation programs as well. PSiO comes with accessories like noise-cancellation headphones, pillow, etc., too.

- https://psio.com/en Use the Ambassador ID "Option29" if you wish to try the product.
- Deep breathing techniques
- Yoga and mindfulness techniques
- Biofeedback
- Spa and sauna
- Water therapy
- Hot tub soaks
- Music and sound therapy
- Massage therapy
- Self-massage routines with Ayurvedic oils

Books:

- Let Food Be Your Medicine: Dietary Changes Proven to Prevent and Reverse Disease by Dr. Don Colbert
- Love your body by Louise Hay
- Healthy Healing By Dr. Linda Page
- Rosemary Gladstar's Medicinal Herbs: A Beginner's Guide
- You Can Heal Your Life by Lousie Hay

- Medical Medium Series of Books by Anthony William
- The Emotion Code by Dr. Bradley Nelson
- Ayurvedic Cooking for Self-Healing by Dr. Vasant Lad
- Aromatherapy for Self-care by Sarah Swanberg

Movies & Documentaries:

- Heal by Director Kelly Noonan
- I am by Director Tom Shadyac
- PGS The Movie by Bill Bennett
- The Story of God with Morgan Freeman
- The Secret by Director Drew Heriot
- Brené Brown: The Call to Courage
- Rewired by Dr. Joe Dispenza
- Secret of Water by Director Jirka Rysavy and Saida Medvedeva
- Samadhi: Maya, the Illusion of the Self by Director Daniel Schmidt

HEALING THE MIND

This section includes managing, rewiring, and changing the thought-patterns of our Mind. The process may consist of affirmations, mental and guided imagery, mind movies, visualization, meditation, journaling, and loving oneself.

Psychological Techniques:

- Hypnosis
- Hypnotherapy
- Heart-centered Hypnotherapy®
- Gestalt Therapy
- Psychodrama Work

- Past-life regression
- Psychotherapies
- NLP therapy
- Tapping Therapy (Emotional Freedom Technique, EFT)
- Equine Therapy
- Art Therapy
- EMDR therapy

Support Groups:

- All 12-Step Programs
- Insight Meditation Center Support Groups
- Loving Relationship Training
- Personal Growth Workshops

Books:

- The Emotion Code
- The Biology of Belief
- Daring Greatly by Brené Brown
- Outwitting The Devil by Napoleon Hill
- Think and Grow Rich for Women by Sharon Lechter
- Becoming Supernatural by Dr. Joe Dispenza
- The Four Agreements by Don Miguel Ruiz

HEALING THE HEART & SOUL

Tools & Programs:

- Gratitude Journal: Living an Intentional Life by Audra McMahon
- Awaken Your Inner Abundance 21-day Challenge using Mudras, Mantras, and Meditation

- Shamanic Retreats
- Plant Medicine Retreats
- Meditation Retreats
- Yoga Retreats
- Nature Retreats
- Creative Retreats that birth your soulful projects and help you heal as well
- LifeMapReading.com

Books:

- The 5 Love Languages: The Secret to Love that Lasts by Dr. Gary Chapman
- The Universe Has Your Back: Transform Fear to Faith by Gabrielle Bernstein
- The Self-Love Workbook: A Life-Changing Guide to Boost Self-Esteem, Recognize Your Worth and Find Genuine Happiness by Dr. Shainna Ali
- Warrior Goddess Training: Become the Woman You Are Meant to Be by HeatherAsh Amara
- Healing the Whole Man Handbook: Effective Prayers for Body, Soul, and Spirit by Joan Hunter

HEALING THROUGH THE SPIRIT

This section includes learning to ask for what you want and expecting miracles in your life. Forgiveness, Receiving, Allowing your Divine/Spiritual connection's presence to enter into your life to heal you, Accepting, Surrendering, Trusting, and Improving Your Intuition.

Spiritual Group Work:

- Unity Churches and Spiritual Centers
- The Church of Religious Science
- Self-Realization Work
- Ananda.org
- Building Your Self-esteem Workshops
- The Art of Living Foundation
- International Center for Reiki Training
- Baha'i Foundation
- 3HO Healthy, Happy, Holy Organization
- Kripalu Center
- Transcendental Meditation (TM)
- The Kabbalah Centre
- Isha Foundation
- Insight Meditation Center

Divination Tools & Alternative Methodologies:

- Oracle Card decks
- Tarot Cards
- Dowsing pendulums
- Zi Wei Dou Shu Life Map Reading
- Chakra Healing & Energy Work
- Qi Men Dun Jia Forecasting
- Personal Feng Shui Alignment based on your Destiny Charts

Note: Option29.org recommends and suggests professionals and local businesses who offer holistic healing services. We also have referral partnerships for our clients and readers to work virtually with professionals we vouch for. Gagan Sarkaria is a soulful life and high achievement coach who offers customized, results-driven, holistic healing, and manifesting abundance programs. If you choose to work with her, please mention **Option29** during your discovery session to get a discount.

“Vulnerability sounds like truth and feels like courage. Truth and courage aren’t always comfortable, but they’re never the weakness.

—Brené Brown

ABOUT THE AUTHOR

AUDRA MCMAHON

Audra McMahon is a powerful speaker and financial literacy expert. She brings almost 2 decades of expertise in the Mortgage industry. She is uncompromisingly focused on helping her clients get a handle on their finances. Audra is a Certified Mortgage Planning Specialist (CMPS), and a Certified Divorce Lending Professional (CDLP). She is also the Founder of Option29.org, an organization committed to helping people navigate through the pain and ambiguity of separation and divorce.

With Audra and her team, you get a formidable force behind you, to guide and support you through your transition in and after divorce. Many rippling effects linger years following a divorce. If known during the divorce, you can wrap it up more quickly and cost-effectively. You are often unaware of the unknows. That pain in the unknown is the motivation and inspiration behind Option29.org and this workbook.

Audra does not want anyone to feel the same horror, confusion, or insecurity that she felt when she divorced. She genuinely wants to protect you. Knowledge is power, and this workbook is just the next step in the right direction.

Audra McMahon brings ambitious results, influential leadership, positive coaching, and financial expertise in budgeting, mortgage, and transition during divorce through community connection and real-life experiences to every client, audience, project, and challenge.

"My great hope is to laugh as much as I cry; to get my work done and try to love somebody and have the courage to accept the love in return.

—Maya Angelou, American Poet

“No one saves us but ourselves.
No one can, and no one may.
We must walk the path.

—Buddha

Option29.org

SERVICES

Coaching:

Our coaching services bring in a holistic approach to your life. We walk you through your significant transition in life for as little as 1-month and up to 12-month timeframes.

Consulting:

At Option29.org, we work with your existing team as needed in all walks of your life.

Preparing For Divorce: Financial Health Assessment Do-it-yourself Workbook:

This workbook is when you are not ready to engage in official professional services but want to educate, plan, and prepare yourself for a significant transition in your life.

Gratitude Journal—Living an Intentional Life:

A daily, directed guide that allows you to focus, plan, and create your thriving life, full of purpose and well-being.

Money Mindset Course:

This is a 2-hour private, one-on-one, review of your current financial situation and guidance on achieving unique personal goals toward financial independence.

Pro Se Assistance:

If you have no children, no property, and no money for an attorney, our team at Option29.org can provide the steps you'll need to handle a divorce yourself. We will help you gather, review, and translate the legal paperwork, then notarize your official files before you can turn them into the court.

"Life begins at the end of your comfort zone.

—Neale Donald Walsch, American Author